This book
belongs to:

God Is Watching Over You

Originally published by iCharacter as two separate books under the titles
Psalm 121 and *Safe with God (Psalm 91)*.
Published by arrangement with iCharacter Limited (Ireland).
www.iCharacter.org

Published by Christian Art Kids, an imprint of Christian Art Publishers,
PO Box 1599, Vereeniging, 1930, RSA

© 2019
First edition 2019

Illustrated by Agnes de Bezenac

Scripture quotations are taken from the *Holy Bible*, New Living Translation®, copyright © 1996, 2004, 2007, 2013, 2015 by Tyndale House Foundation. Used by permission of Tyndale House Publishers, Inc., Carol Stream, Illinois 60188. All rights reserved.

Printed in China

ISBN 978-1-4321-2940-8

19 20 21 22 23 24 25 26 27 28 – 10 9 8 7 6 5 4 3 2 1

Printed in Shenzhen, China
January 2019
Print Run: 100439

GOD IS WATCHING OVER YOU

When no one is around,
is there help? I pray and
the Lord comes to help me.

I look up to the mountains—
does my help come from there?
My help comes from the Lord ...

(Psalm 121:1-2)

He has made everything
in heaven and on earth.

... who made heaven and earth!

(Psalm 121:2)

He will protect me
from getting hurt.
He never stops looking
out for me.

He will not let you stumble;
the One who watches over you
will not slumber.

(Psalm 121:3)

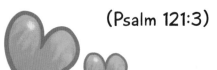

The Lord takes care of His people. He never sleeps or takes a break.

Indeed, He who watches over Israel never slumbers or sleeps.

(Psalm 121:4)

The Lord
makes sure I am safe.

The Lord Himself

watches over you!

(Psalm 121:5)

He is like
a shadow that
never leaves
my side.

The Lord
stands beside you
as your protective shade.

(Psalm 121:5)

The Lord guards me in the heat of the day.

The sun will not harm you by day...

(Psalm 121:6)

And the Lord guards me
under the light
of the moon at night.

...nor the moon at night.

(Psalm 121:6)

The Lord will be with me
when danger is near. He watches
me from the time I am born
until I grow old.

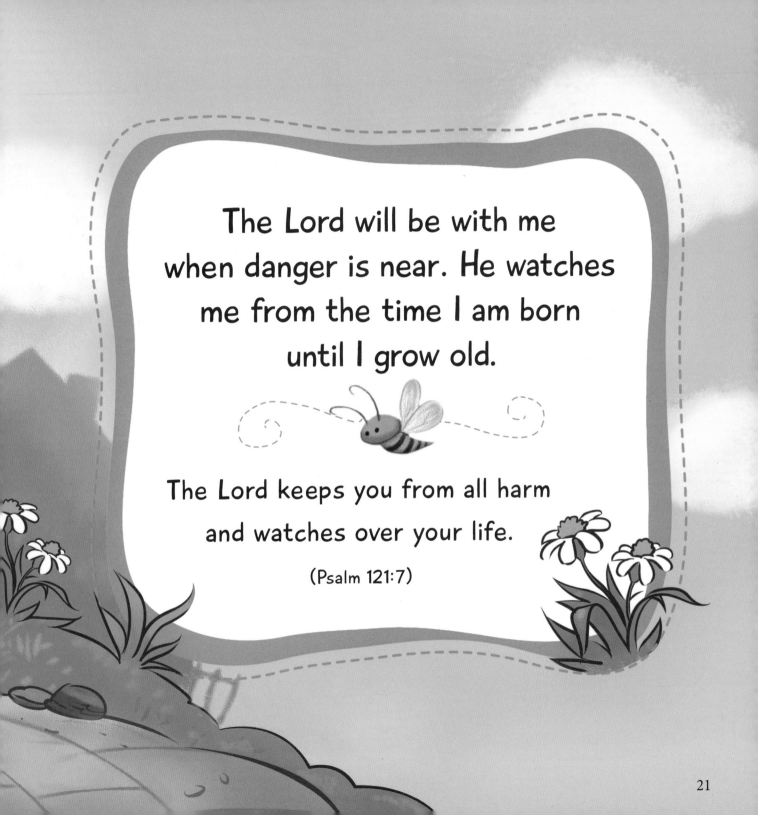

The Lord keeps you from all harm
and watches over your life.

(Psalm 121:7)

The Lord knows
when I go out and when I come
home. He's here with me now,
and will stay with me always.

The Lord keeps watch over you as you
come and go both now and forever.

(Psalm 121:8)

When I stay close
to the Lord, I can rest
and be at peace.

Those who live in the
shelter of the Most High will
find rest in the shadow
of the Almighty.

(Psalm 91:1)

I know that
I can trust the Lord,
because He protects me
and makes me strong.

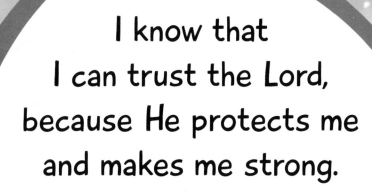

This I declare about the Lord:
He alone is my refuge, my place
of safety; He is my God,
and I trust Him.

(Psalm 91:2)

The Lord can
protect me from those
who want to hurt me,
and He can keep me healthy.

For He will rescue you from
every trap and protect you from
deadly disease.

(Psalm 91:3)

The Lord covers me,
like a bird covers its baby.
He guards me faithfully.

He will cover you with His feathers.
He will shelter you with His wings.
His faithful promises are
your armor and protection.

(Psalm 91:4)

I don't have to be afraid of the dark, or of anything during the day.

Do not be afraid of the terrors of the night, nor the arrow that flies in the day.

(Psalm 91:5)

I don't have
to fear sickness, because
the Lord is with me.

Do not dread the disease
that stalks in darkness,
nor the disaster that
strikes at midday.

(Psalm 91:6)

Get well
soon !

35

Even if there is war
or chaos all around me,
I can feel safe with the Lord. I see
what happens to those who do wrong
things, so I don't want to copy them.

Though a thousand fall at your side, though
ten thousand are dying around you, these
evils will not touch you. Just open
your eyes, and see how the
wicked are punished.

(Psalm 91:7-8)

The Lord protects me like
a fortress, so when I am with Him,
nothing can harm me.

If you make the Lord your refuge,
if you make the Most High your shelter,
no evil will conquer you; no plague
will come near your home.

(Psalm 91:9-10)

The Lord tells His angels to be my bodyguards wherever I go. They watch over me, so I don't get hurt.

For He will order His angels to protect you wherever you go. They will hold you up with their hands so you won't even hurt your foot on a stone.

(Psalm 91:11-12)

The Lord's angels are strong enough
to help me even in dangerous places.
The Lord loves me, and I love Him.
That's why He wants to keep me safe.

You will trample upon lions and cobras; you will
crush fierce lions and serpents under your feet!
The Lord says, "I will rescue those who love Me.
I will protect those who trust in My name."

(Psalm 91:13-14)

The Lord
says that when I
pray and call out to
Him, that He will come
and rescue me.

" When they call on Me, I will answer;
I will be with them in trouble.
I will rescue and
honor them."

(Psalm 91:15)

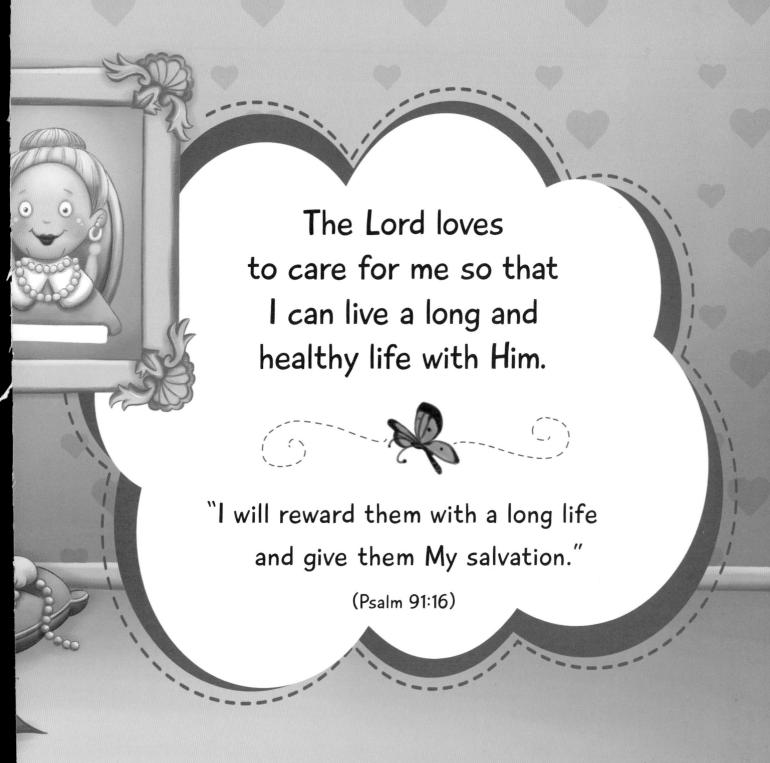

The Lord loves
to care for me so that
I can live a long and
healthy life with Him.

"I will reward them with a long life
and give them My salvation."

(Psalm 91:16)

Always remember
that God is with you.
He cares for you
and always
watches over you.